MARKETING

GUIDES

for Small Businesses:

REPUTATION

MANAGEMENT

Ken Tucker | Ray L. Perry | Phil Singleton

Marketing Guides for Small Businesses: Reputation Management

www.ducttapepublishing.com

FOREWORD

Thoughts on using this guide

Since you've opened this guide I'm guessing you want to grow your business, get better at marketing or maybe just figure out how to acquire that first customer.

So, first off – congratulations. A commitment to life-long learning is the hallmark of any truly committed entrepreneur.

But make no mistake, there is more information available than time to consume it and it's very important that you take in a steady diet of practical information created by those that have been where you're trying to go.

This guide certainly meets that criteria.

I know the authors of this guide personally and have seen their work first-hand. They not only consistently deliver results for their clients; both have been very generous in sharing their knowledge by way of training fellow members of the Duct Tape Marketing Consultant Network. I think this speaks volumes because it allows me to confidently assure you that you are about to read some pretty good stuff.

Ken Tucker, Ray L. Perry, and Phil Singleton are three rock star marketing professionals in the Duct Tape Marketing Consultant Network. As certified marketing consultants they:

Have completed my intensive training program;
Participate in ongoing marketing training and mentoring;

Have exclusive access to an arsenal of proven tools and methodologies;
Are members of an elite, fast-growing global network of talented small business marketing consultants;
Are certified to install the Duct Tape Marketing System.

At Duct Tape Marketing, we teach that strategy before tactics is the key to creating a winning, high ROI marketing plan. Getting your strategy right from the get-go is the only way to create a web-centric, inbound marketing platform that will consistently draw ideal customers to your doorstep.

Once you get the right strategy in place, however, tactical execution is the only way to ensure that your marketing plan will produce results.

The *Marketing Guides* series is broken down into logical book chunks, and in a practical, easy-to-read format. Each book in this series will give you - the business owner - the education you need to understand and apply an important tactic to your business.

I highly recommend this Book and the entire Marketing Guides series. Read this Book, apply what you learn and there is no question your business will generate more business and more leads. Period.

John Jantsch
Author Of *Duct Tape Marketing*
www.DuctTapeMarketing.com

TABLE OF CONTENTS

INTRODUCTION

You know your reputation matters. You spend the time and effort it takes to keep your customers happy and coming back for more. You provide a top quality service or product, excellent customer service, and rarely have a problem you can't resolve. Your reputation is worth its weight in gold and you work hard to keep it shining.

The trouble is it takes just one dissatisfied customer with access to the Internet to change everything. Add in the fact that most satisfied customers don't take the time to review at all, and that one complaint becomes damaging to your business. Few things go viral as quickly as a complaint on the web.

The organic, consumer-led review process results in far more negative reviews than positive ones. Unhappy customers tell an average of 24 people about their experience; happy ones only tell 15 people. Did you know four out of five consumers have reversed a purchase decision based on negative online reviews? Responding to both positive and negatives reviews with authentic responses, not cookie-cutter answers, will improve your reputation.

But online reputation management is more complicated than just having good manners in how you deal with your customers, and eating the occasional crow sandwich when your best intentions fall short. The pool of entrepreneurs seems to be well-represented by hotheads – and that fire in the belly is a bit of a necessary characteristic considering all that our ventures demand from us. As a small business owner, it's justifiable that you'd feel strongly about the quality of the products or services you provide. You might even feel strongly enough to bring some heat to your reaction to someone slamming you online or offline.

Don't do that. Don't let your emotions take over when you perceive a threat to your hard-earned reputation. There are so many harmful ways you can react to reputation issues. Just a few common missteps:

Losing your cool and either getting defensive or going on the offense. You want to clear your name. You want an apology. You want, at least, the opportunity to tell your side of the story. But if you go after a detractor, it will almost assuredly backfire. If you think that customer's angry now, just imagine what could happen if your response appears to question or attack them.

Burying your head in the sand. You simply can't ignore or outrun reputation problems. Hiding is not an option.

Publishing fake reviews. Wrong in so many ways – but also understandably tempting. After all, money talks. Buying fake reviews might seem like a sure way to control what's published. However, if you get caught – and you will – the fallout from a failed attempt to game the system is so bad that you'll regret ever having the "brilliant" idea to try it.

Turning a deaf ear to your customers. Customers can be some of the most unreasonable people on the planet. They're quick to complain, slow to appreciate your efforts, and very rarely extend the sort of grace you've come to find justifiable after so many years in business. It seems like a ridiculous waste of resources to provide the infrastructure and resources needed to listen to customers. Why pay to hear complaints? But plugging your ears with your fingers is a blunder that can cost you.

Hitting the delete button. Oh, so tempting when you get a nasty-gram either via email or on your social media. While simply making the problem disappear with a click might give you some instant relief, it's certain to ignite a fury in your detractor that takes on a life of its own.

Failing to stake a claim on your own territory. Identity theft is not just about a hacker getting your credit card number and buying a block of tickets to an upcoming concert. It happens to companies, too – especially those with somewhat generic names. You can end up with a reputation challenge by virtue of mistaken identity or outright identity theft. It's possible to protect yourself, but that protection won't happen without concerted effort.

But, the root of the problem is not necessarily in a bad reaction to a reputation challenge. The bigger problem is in failing to take a proactive role in monitoring, managing, and marketing your reputation.

Every business needs to set up and implement processes for listening to what's being said – and knowing how to respond in ways that bring you out on top rather than dragging you down in public. But you also need to take steps now, before your reputation ever comes under fire, to build a hedge of protection around your online reputation. We'll talk about both in this short guide.

Can you see why online reputation management just hit the top of your to-do list? Start by asking satisfied customers to give you a good review. Make it easy for them. Direct them to an easy-to-use review process and they will help you build your business.

We'll dig into the hows and whys here, and you'll come away with a solid basic understanding of how to protect the reputation you've built with your own blood, sweat, and tears. You can't ignore the importance of this marketing initiative – but with some work and know-how, you can not only protect your business' reputation, you can also leverage it to bring in more new customers, too.

CHAPTER 1

WHAT IS ONLINE REPUTATION MANAGEMENT?

Online reputation management is the process of taking control over what someone sees when they Google your name or business. You may think that what your customers post about your business is out of your hands, but it's not. You have the ability to influence what information shows up, especially negative information.

Online reputation management can help move positive information to the top of the search engine results and push negative information farther down. While you can't remove negative comments from the Internet, you can push them off the first page of search engine results so they aren't as visible to potential customers. Most people make their buying decisions based on the top two or three results, so this change can be all you need to improve your online reputation.

Social media plays a major role in online reputation management. Social media moves fast, so when customers use social media to communicate with your brand, they expect a quick response. According to Brandwatch.com, a leading online reputation management service, 53% of customers on Twitter who ask a brand a question expect to receive a response within one hour. If their comment is a complaint, that number jumps to a whopping 72%. While the results of their study showed that 65% of companies respond within 24 hours, only 11.2% of retail brands met that one-hour expectation.

With numbers like that, it is easy to understand why you need to take a proactive role in your online reputation management.

Let's Get Started. Google Yourself.

The first step in taking control of your online presence is to learn what's out there. Start by searching Google for your name and your business name. Before you can get a clear picture of results others are seeing, you need to sign out of any Google account.

Now, type in exactly what people call you. Search for misspelled versions of your name as well. See what people are saying. Search for:

- Business name
- Personal name
- Any common nicknames
- Any common misspellings of your name
- Any incorrect information, such as wrong address or wrong hours of operation

Examine the Results

Look through the results, especially on the first page. Look for duplicate mentions of the same problem. This might include a tweet that gets retweeted, a Facebook status that keeps getting shares and comments or (worse) more than one person upset about the same thing. The goal here is to get the full picture of your online reputation.

As you find mentions of your name or business, sort them into one of these four piles: Negative, Neutral, Not Me, and Positive.

- Negative posts are critical to find. Whether it's a photo flaunting you in an unflattering light, a negative remark from a bitter ex-friend, a total lie, or a former employee complaint, put it in this category. Negative posts are a high priority class, and you need to address them as soon as possible.

- Neutral posts are still about you, but they don't add anything to the conversation. Neutral posts might include your embarrassing stint in the dunk tank at the festival last summer, your grandma's sugar cookie recipe posted on Pinterest or your softball team's last place ranking last season. Sure, these silly posts might make you look a little foolish. The good news is they don't hurt your online reputation.

- Not Me posts are mistaken identity posts. These people have the same name as you, but they aren't you. Unfortunately, when they show up on the search engine result page (SERP), they will add to the public's first impression of you.

- Positive posts are just that. Positive. Customers who review you in a favorable manner, well thought-out, branded content, and photos of personal and business successes are all considered positive posts. We love this category. The number one tool to combat any reputation issue is to make sure this category is always overflowing with good things you say and do.

At this point, you should be getting a realistic picture of your online reputation. How are you doing? Did you find a lot of information? What about those negatives? Did you have any surprises? Let's break things down a bit as we look at the steps you can take to build or restore your online reputation.

CHAPTER 2

YOUR REPUTATION'S STARTING POINT

What's your online reputation's current status? Based on what you discovered through the research you just did, put yourself into one of three categories.

- **You're a Nobody.** Did you just find out you have no content at all? Now you know exactly where to start.

- **You're the Bad Guy.** Find out it's not looking pretty? It's okay. At least now you are in a position to change things for the better, so buck up and let's get to work.

- **You're a Superhero.** Find some good stuff in danger of losing page one in the SERPs? No problem. You'll learn how to make your quality content climb right to the top of the page, where everyone will see it.

Become a Somebody

Start at the beginning. Set up a website for your business if you don't already have one. Buy a domain name using your actual name or your company name. Purchase the domain name for as long a period as you can. If you claim your domain name for an extended period, such as three years, it shows you are making a commitment to this name and are likely to be a serious business owner. Get your domain name in the .com version if possible or .net if it isn't.

Try not to change your name to fit the domain options. If your name is Suzie Serious-Business Owner, and the .com version is not available, it is better to choose .net than choose Susan Business Owner.

Once you have your domain name, set up hosting and install a WordPress blog. WordPress is SEO friendly with a few easy-to-install custom plugins.

- **Create a Home Page**. The goal here is to make sure prospective customers who land on your website know they're in the right place – that you understand what they need and can provide solutions for the problems that sent them your way in the first place. Be sure to focus on your customers rather than yourself.

- **Create a Products or Services Page**. You can create one for each product or service you sell, but if you're just starting out, it's fine to have a single page that presents them all. Show each product or service, talk about the benefits your customers get and provide ample details. Practice your SEO here as well. For instance, rather than "My Products", title the page "[Your Name] Products and Services."

- **Create a Contact Page**. Make sure it's easy for a prospective customer to reach you. Include a contact form rather than listing an email address to cut down on spam messages. Always include a phone number, as well as links to your company's social media profiles.

- **Create a Review Funnel Page**. Make it easy for people to provide a positive online review. Ninety percent of U.S. purchasers read online reviews, but only six percent write them. Happy customers don't write reviews because they think the process will be time-consuming and tedious, or they simply forget. When you make the process easy and put the option right in front of your customers, they will be more likely to offer a review.

  Google Reviews uses a free tool from Grade.us called the Google Review Link Generator. This little tool will create a link you can use to direct people to a landing page for Google Reviews. Go to the Google Review Link Generator and put in your information. Confirm it is correct. Choose your options. Just like that, a spot opens for people to leave a review on your page.

- **Make Sure Your Review Page is Mobile-Friendly**. According to Statista, the number of people using smartphones worldwide was at 1.5 billion in 2014; forecasts expect that number to go as high as 2.5 billion by 2019. Modern Comment, a social media promotion expert, reports that 63% of individuals who do local searches are likely to buy within one hour. Making sure every part of your website is mobile friendly is critical to success.

Time for Your Social Life

Set up a social media profile on at least three social media platforms, i.e. Facebook, Twitter, Pinterest, LinkedIn, YouTube, Google+, etc. Fill out the profiles as completely as possible. Use the name your customers call you; for instance, if your name is Peter but your customers call you Pete, the latter is what you should use.

Make sure each profile links back to your website. Link profiles to each other when and where possible. Create prominent links on your website that take customers to all your social media profiles.

Social media is a great place to interact with your audience. Though you are promoting a product, you can still feel free to post cute little things that engage your customers. Perhaps throw out a random question that has nothing to do with business: "What's your favorite ice cream?" "If you were a crayon, what color would you be?" See if you can get people to answer. If they do, respond.

You can also share small pieces of valued information through social media with an encouragement to visit your website. Create a pleasant, helpful presence, and then spread the love around.

If you're convinced you won't have the time, that's no problem. There are several tools available, both free and paid, to create a cache of social media content and schedule it to post at a time of your choosing. You can put together content for the entire week, on several platforms, in a couple of hours. You will still need to spend a bit of live time on your pages for the best effect, and respond appropriately, but you can post around the clock with relative ease.

Social media is the fastest growing form of communication out there. Marketing and advertising have taken on a whole new look since the days of posting a sales page with an opt-in at the bottom. People expect and demand a personalized presence in an online world.

What If You're the Accidental Bad Guy?

You did your research, and discovered your reputation is less than what you want. There are some photos from an eventful office party, one vocal unhappy customer from six months ago or a link to a traffic ticket last October. It's time to make it go away. The goal is to bury the negative remark.

How to Negate the Negatives

Take a look at the meat of the negative comment. Is the complaint valid? Is there a problem with your product, your service or your staff? Be honest with yourself. This critical look is even more important if you see the same complaint registered more than once.

Use the AAA of online reputation management as a guide: Acknowledge, Apologize, and then make Amends. Acknowledge the problem and your ownership of it, apologize for the problem, and do everything you can to make amends.

The Best and Worst Things to Do

The best possible step you can take for your online reputation is to fix the problem. Do everything you can to resolve the issue for the unhappy customer or client. Is there a shipping problem? Ship another one at your cost. Is there a customer service problem? Take the matter in hand. Contact the customer and deal with it. Don't be afraid to apologize.

Make sure you return to wherever the negative comment appeared and offer a public reply. Here's where the rubber meets the road: you need to show public ownership of the problem and a willingness to fix it without a hint of arrogance.

You've already contacted the unhappy customer and made things right. Now, respond in the same platform where you took the hit. If you resolved the issues and things go your way, even a little bit, you might even get a response from your now-happy customer acknowledging the resolution.

This kind of negative content doesn't have to harm you. When people see you took the necessary steps to fix the problem and did so with integrity, you'll gain some supporters.

One of the worst things you can do is slough off the responsibility to someone else. After all, if they work for you, they represent you, and you are responsible. It's surprising how much gets resolved by the simple transparency of admitting a mistake and apologizing for it. Combine this attitude with the steps necessary to right the wrong and things are looking up.

Here's the Troublemaker

Other types of negative comments include negative reviews, negative media coverage, and even hate sites. These types of negative posts can cause problems for your business. If someone Googles your company to learn who you are and immediately find defamatory information, they are most likely to give their business to someone else.

Negative articles, including online reviews, can hit hard. Your company risks losing a sizeable chunk of potential customers for every single negative report they see. If you've got a few negative reviews, the potential loss balloons exponentially.

But there are ways of making the ugly content move out of your way. Always remember: the most important page of the search engine results is the first page. Few people scroll beyond that. In fact, most won't scroll beyond the first few items.

We live in a hurry-up world. People are more likely to use their mobile phone or tablet to access the Internet than any other device. Most won't scroll down the page on their phones more than once or twice at the most. Some users are unlikely to scroll at all. Keep your focus on page one of Google, because that is where people are looking. That's also what we're going to look at in the next chapter.

CHAPTER 3

MOVE YOUR SERP RESULTS

The trick is Search Engine Optimization. You thought there was going to be a magic button? Sorry, that's not the way it works. You must put in aggressive SEO content work. Put out great content. Write blog posts offering genuine value to the reader. You are an expert in your field, so demonstrate your expertise online.

The best way to gain an audience online is to operate on the Know-Like-Trust principle. Here's how it works: You want people to do business with you. You want them to spend their hard-earned money buying what you are selling, whether that's a product or a service. People spend their money with those they know, like and trust. Your job is to make sure they get to know you in a way that makes them like and trust you. The fastest way to do that is to give them some of what they need for free.

Everyone loves a gift. Think back to your last birthday. Did you get any gifts? Along with the obligatory tie or Mani/Pedi gift certificate, did you get a truly valuable gift – something that made a difference in your day-to-day life? Imagine how nice it is to go out to a fancy dinner. You are escorted to your table, waited on hand and foot and fed an elegant, delightful meal. After you finish eating, you sip a steaming hot cup of delicious coffee and indulge in a free piece of the richest, creamiest cheesecake outside of New York City. That's a gift.

Now, imagine receiving the gift of a full-service, all-expenses paid chef for a year. 365 days and nights filled with nutritious, mouth-watering food and drink, complete with the kitchen cleanup included. THAT can be a life-changer. Think of the time and energy you could save to spend on family, or work, or fun? Think of the lifestyle change you could accomplish if you had an entire year of nutritious eating with none of the hassles. Now, this is value. That's what you need to provide to your customers without charging them a dime.

Give them useful information they can use to better their lives, improve their finances, grow their business, save time, or increase their recreational activities. You can achieve this by learning how to optimize content for the Internet.

What Is SEO?

Search Engine Optimization makes your content as search engine friendly as possible. SEO uses keywords or specific words targeted to your business. By placing these keywords throughout your content, you can give the Google spiders roaming the Internet a "heads up" to find it. You will also link your content to credible databases and directories across the web.

Proper SEO includes researching the keywords people type in when they use search engines to find a business like yours. There are tools available to help you drill down on which keywords are more valuable or easiest to rank in the search engines. Place those targeted words and phrases in your title and H1 (header) content. Use a variation of them in subheadings throughout. Keywords are also beneficial in the call-to-action, the part where you tell them to call or click now.

Is That All There Is to It?

Not even close. There is a whole other category of SEO known as Local SEO. Local SEO involves making sure you have all your pertinent information in the right places. The most important information about your business is your NAP: Name, address and phone number. You should have this information listed wherever you can. Make sure you are listed in online directories like Yelp and the Better Business Bureau.

Google has two important places to register your business. The first is Google My Business. Click into this site and add your business NAP. Make sure all your information is correct and then beef it up. This action will get you updated on Google Search and Google Maps. People can see your hours, contact information and more. Include pictures that prove the unique qualities of your business. Showcase what makes you stand out from others. You can even do a virtual tour if that fits with what you do.

Google My Business will also let you know how and where customers found you. This information helps you direct your marketing dollars where they do the most good. Google My Business doesn't cost you a dime, making it worth its weight in gold.

When you update your listing in Google My Business, Google also puts your information on Google Maps. This step is becoming more important as Google narrows the winners on their SERP pages. Known as the Google Local Pack, last year Google restricted its most prominent search results to seven listings with map views closest to the searcher. Recently they shortened that list to only three businesses, making it tougher than ever to rank on page one of a Google search. One of those three listings is a paid listing, so in reality there are only two organic, local listings. Having at least five 5-star online reviews can help your business make the cut.

Every place connecting the same name, address and phone number adds a piece of Internet real estate to your business. Using the same accurate information is critical to maintaining consistency. Put your social media icons wherever you can on these other sites as well as on your website.

Know These Five Facts about SEO:
1. There are many tactics and techniques involved in SEO content. Many businesses find the best way to keep on top of the ever-changing algorithms is to hire this out to an agency or a freelancer who specializes in optimizing content.

2. Be very careful to use legitimate strategies and tactics. Do not stuff your content full of keywords; it won't help your page rank. While strategic placement of keywords is important, awkward placement just for the sake of using a particular word is not beneficial. In fact, Google might penalize you for it.

3. Cloaking is a "black-hat" SEO tactic to avoid. In the simplest terms, cloaking directs the spiders on the search engine to see something other than what is actually on the page. It's done by manipulating the data in the HTML code and showing certain keywords to the robots. It can get your site banned from Google. The good news about cloaking is if you don't understand how to do it, you aren't doing it by accident. It's a bit tricky, and it's intentional.

4. Finally, just say no to buying, farming or trading links. Make sure every single link is either coming from or going to an actual, legitimate site connected to you and your business. Link to high-quality blogs, products, news sites and social media profiles of real people. No long-

term progress results from bypassing legitimacy and giving a false sense of interaction and impact.

5. Last word on "black hat" SEO: If someone promises you immediate SEO results, it's not legitimate. If you want real results, put in the work and expect two to six months (or more) to start seeing the change.

Like anything of value, solid SEO isn't built overnight. While there are no shortcuts, there are best practices you should learn and follow. The tricky thing about SEO is that best practices are constantly shifting and evolving – so you can't just learn it once and leave it alone.

Next up, we'll talk about a couple of ways you can improve your own website's standing with the search engines. One is by piggybacking on other prominent, authoritative websites, and the other is by expanding your own site's digital footprint.

CHAPTER 4

CONTENT PROTECTS AND BOOSTS YOUR REPUTATION

No doubt you've heard so many people singing the praises of content marketing that you've either jumped on board that train or banned the C-word from your premises. Content is a beast. It's a beast you can reign and rule, and then climb on its shoulders to stand out from the crowd in your marketplace. It's also a beast that never stops eating. You never, ever have "enough" content.

Aside from using engaging, educational content to squash your sales cycle and help your customers come to know, like, and trust you, your content efforts can also help with your online reputation. That goes for content you post on your own site and on other websites, too.

A Good Offense Makes a Powerful Defense

Content marketing allows you to tell your story the way you want it told. Tell it well enough, often enough, and in the ways the search engines respect, and you'll move upward on the search engine results pages. You'll position yourself as an expert and build valuable credibility for your business. This positioning can help to insulate you from online reputation challenges.

Your content marketing strategy should include text, images, and videos. It's a little like playing the board game Monopoly. The more search engine results page slots you can control, the less room you leave for damaging reputation digs on the first page. Remember, people rarely scroll past the first page when they go looking for the products and services you sell.

Align Yourself with the Giants

It used to be that you never wanted to link outward from content on your website. You just wanted to keep website visitors on your site as long as possible. Back then, the only good link was an inbound link. Now it's a bit different. You still want to keep them engaged with your content, but you can also borrow some credibility from big names that are relevant to your content.

Your content should feature an outbound link or two for each page, connecting with an authority website that makes sense for the topic you're covering. Google's looking for the best possible user experience, and now sees that kind of outbound link as valuable. Don't go overboard, of course.

Getting a relevant, high-quality inbound link from an authority site isn't likely to happen – if you're relying on being mentioned or highlighted in their content.

However, you can still sometimes get a good backlink by taking matters into your own hands.

Look for prominent websites that accept regular comments – and leave a thoughtful, valuable comment in a relevant discussion. Include your website address in your comment if possible. Some of the best authority sites have domains that end in .gov or .edu. Look on the community pages of your local government or college alma mater for articles you can offer beneficial commentary on, along with a link to your website or profile. Find out if your Chamber of Commerce has a website and get on any lists offered to local businesses.

Get Your Blog Going

Producing a regular blog is one of the most reliable ways to influence your page rankings and online credibility. Google loves to rank fresh, relevant content and the best way to introduce new content is through a blog on your website.

A blog is also an excellent way to show your expertise in your field. By sharing useful information, you establish yourself as credible, knowledgeable and capable. Your audience will begin to seek you out when they need an answer for their problem. You can increase the strength of this reputation by anticipating your target market's problem and providing a solution immediately. Your blog is the place to do that.

CHAPTER 5

TOOLS TO HELP YOU KEEP TABS

There are dozens of different tools you can use to monitor your online reputation. Let's take a look at some of the most popular options.

- **Google Alerts.** You can use Google to set up an alert for your name, your business name, or the name(s) of your products. Once the alert is set up, Google will notify you when someone mentions you online. This little tool will help you respond in a timely manner to any comments or mentions of your business name.

  When the comments are positive, your response, which includes a link back to your website, becomes a piece of helpful SERP ranking. If the comments are negative, especially if they refer to a problem, Google Alerts allows you to respond immediately and take the necessary steps to solve the problem. This prevents the opportunity for the issue to gain traction and cause you real problems.

- Trackur provides both free and paid services in social media monitoring. This is especially good for finding out if influential people are talking about your brand. While most small businesses don't need to concern themselves with high-visibility people discussing them online, it's not hard to understand how influential people in your industry have the power to make or break you. Trackur has a metric that will gauge the power of any particular commenter in percentage form, so you can tell if a power voice is mentioning your brand.

- Social media monitoring sites include Social Mention, Mention, and Hootsuite. Other common ones include Klout, Crowdfire, Buffer, BuzzSumo, Keyhole, and SproutSocial.

Your Most Important Media Is Social Media

It's impossible to overstate the power of social media when it comes to reputation management. This ever-increasing series of platforms has given power to the people like never before when it comes to praising or bashing the companies they patronize. Learning to respond and problem-solve on the fly is a critical customer service skill in our online business world.

People want to know that you're human. Although we love interacting online from the privacy of our computer or smartphone, we also want to know we are dealing with real individuals when things don't turn out the way we had hoped. People don't like feeling like a number. They want and expect, fast, empathetic and personal attention.

Respond to problems on the platform where the complaint appeared. When a customer jumps on Twitter to state their grievance, respond right away through that medium rather than asking them to email or call. If the conversation becomes lengthy you may be able to better serve your customer through another means of communication, but acknowledging the problem where they bring it allows for quick and helpful responses that can defuse the situation.

How to Clean Up Your Social Media Accounts

You do have a certain amount of control over your social media accounts. If a negative comment is on your own account, follow these steps to get it out of there.

- Go to your profile page on Facebook, Twitter or LinkedIn. All three give you the option to scroll to a particular post and delete it. Removing the damage is a definite priority.

- Go to the hosting company of the site displaying the offending post. They are not obligated to take it down, but they might if you ask. Paste the URL into www.whoisdomaintools.com to find the registered owner of the site.

- You might have recourse in libel, copyright, or unauthorized personal material laws if you didn't give permission for some content. Start with an email process of requesting a cease and desist, and follow through with a hard copy if needed. At some point, you might even need to consider involving an attorney.

Hopefully, your business will never get into a situation where legal intervention becomes a reasonable option to consider. Nipping reputation challenges in the bud is a far less stressful and more effective way to protect yourself. Next we'll look at some sites that can help you do just that.

CHAPTER 6

ONLINE REVIEW SITES

Online review sites are excellent places to get your business name noticed. You can also add links that will improve your ranking and reputation. People love to buy from places they trust, and one thing that increases trust is a high opinion of someone else, even if that someone is a stranger. Hearing that others have a favorable relationship with your company will ease a customer toward liking and trusting you. Because Know, Like, and Trust are the three steps to clicking the 'buy' button, online review sites are a valuable place to have your website link.

According to a survey by BrightLocal.com, 88% of consumers say they trust online reviews as much as personal recommendations. It's easy to see why positive online reviews are so important. If that doesn't fire you up on the power of online reviews, they also found that 72% of consumers take action after reading a positive review, either by calling your business or visiting your website.

You can ease your customers into writing an online review by making the process easier. One trick is to use the review funnel mentioned earlier. Don't be afraid to remind them to write a review, especially during their downtime. You can send a text message or use an email drip campaign to request they fill out the review. Be sure to include the link to your online review page.

Online reviews are not enough. You need to respond to the reviews as well. According to Modern Comment, 78% of consumers say that seeing management respond to online reviews makes it clear the business cares about them.

Having at least five 5-star reviews can change the mind of even the most skeptical customer. Imagine this scenario: Bob is across town at a meeting but he needs a quick lunch. He pulls out his phone to see what's convenient. As Bob pulls up Yelp, he sees six different options within three blocks. How does he choose? He picks the one with the most five-star ratings or the one that has the highest average rating.

Review sites help consumers avoid making a bad decision about where they go to spend their money. People tend to give honest reviews, no matter what they might say to your face. If you operate in a high competition industry, make sure you're at the top of the review list if you want traffic from sites like Yelp, Google Reviews, Foursquare or Merchant Circle.

Best-selling author and expert in customer service Chip Bell said:

> *"In the customer's mind the clock starts when he or she posts a negative review, and your reputation drops with every hour you delay providing a response. Be honest, be apologetic, and offer the aggrieved customer an easy way to access you. Bad reviews that remain unanswered signal to other customers you are disinterested. It also fuels the perception that the negative report by an angry customer was probably accurate. In the social media world, you are assumed guilty until your response alters public perception."*

Make sure your review page has no other calls to action. You want to keep the customer's focus on filling out the review and not clicking elsewhere.

For a brick and mortar business, consider using a small business card or other takeaway card with a printed invitation asking your customer to provide a review. If your sales are online, you can direct them to your review page on your site after they complete a sale or prepare to leave your website.

You can use more than one review page option, but limit it to just a few. Too many options are confusing. If they can make it simple and log in with Facebook, they are more inclined to do so.

Make sure if a customer is not happy, they have the option to contact you before they post a review. It is always better if they can speak to you rather than leave a negative review that everyone will see.

There are thousands of online review sites. Some of the most popular ones are listed here, with a bit about what type of businesses they include and why you should make sure your business gets on board.

- Angie's List is popular. With over 720 business services listed and more than 3 million users, Angie's List is one of the best places to have your business recognized. Users of this popular membership site input over 60,000 reviews every month. Angie's List caters to local businesses, so it is especially helpful to businesses with a local target market.
- Just like Google My Business is important for your local SEO, Bing Places for Business is a critical site to update with your NAP. Make sure your listing is accurate and consistent with other areas where this information appears.
- FourSquare is a popular review site with many mobile users. A review here will connect you with millions of mobile phone searchers and provide your customers with another place to toot their horns about how much they love you.
- Don't forget Yelp, another popular review site. Asking your satisfied customers to give you a Yelp review will add to your credibility and SERP rankings.

- BrightLocal and Grade.us are both excellent review monitoring sites.

Here is a table of popular review sites, sorted by industry:

Industry	Review Site	Industry	Review Site
Major Review Sites	Google	**Directories**	Angie's List
	Google (tablet or mobile)		BBB
	Yahoo Local		Citysearch
	Yelp		DexKnows
Social Media	Facebook		Insider Pages
	Foursquare		Manta
	Linkedin		Merchantcircle.com
	Twitter		SuperPages.com
Local	BBB	**Auto Car & Dealer**	CarGurus
	EZLocal		Edmunds.com
	Judy's Book		Cars.com
	Rateabiz		Dealer Rater
	Yellowbot	**Auto Repair**	AutoMD
	Tupalo.com		Repair Pal
Chiropractic	Wellness.com	**Dentist**	RateaDentist.com

	UCompareHealthCare		SolutionReach
	RateMDs		Healthgrades
	Vitals		Dr. Oogle
	Healthgrades		Vitals
Education & School	Great Schools	**Elder Care**	Caring.com
	Private School Review		Golden Reviews
	Healthgrades	**Financial Services**	Credit Karma
	Dr. Oogle		Lendingtree
	Vitals		OurParents
Home Services and Residential Contractor	Angie's List	**HealthCare**	Fertility IQ
	Buildzoom		Healthgrades
	Guildquality		Healthy Hearing
	HomeAdvisor		Patient Fusion
	Houzz		RateMDs
	Kudzu		Real Patient Ratings
	Porch		Real Self
	Smith		SolutionReach
	Thumbtack		UCompareHealthCare

Employment	Glassdoor		Vitals
	Indeed		WebMD
Lawyer	Avvo		Wellness
	Lawyers.com		Zocdoc
	Martindale.com	**Hotels & Resorts**	Tripadvisor
Property & Rentals	Flipkey		Fodor's
	HomeAway		Orbitz
	VRBO		Travelocity
Real Estate	Homes.com		Spafinder Wellness 365
	Movoto	**Moving & Movers**	Movers.com
	Realtor.com		MovingcompanyReviews.com
	Trulia		My Moving Reviews
	Zillow	**Salons & Beauty**	Realself
Travel & Hospitality	BedandBreakfast.com		Spafinder
	Booking.com	**Software**	Capterra
	Fodor's		Crowd
	Freetobook		GetApp
	Get Your Guide		Software Advice

	Hostelbookers		TrustRadius
	Hostels.com	**Restaurants**	OpenTable
	Hostelworld		Zomato
	Hostelz.com		Zagat
	LateRooms.com		Tripadvisor
	Tourradar		Beeradvocate
	Tripadvisor		Fodor's
	Viator		Menupages
Product	Amazon		Restaurant.com
	BeerAdvocate		Zagat
	Consumer Affairs	**Wedding Industry**	The Knot
	Etsy		WeddingWire
	Goodreads		
	IMDb		
	Reevoo		

Keep in mind that it is important to have the reviews written on sites that matter to the search engines – especially Google My Business and Yelp – as well as the sites that matter to the searcher, namely industry specific sites like Zillow, HealthGrades, or Avvo.

There are some serves that do a great job of collecting reviews of your business, but they might now help you show up in local search results. It's almost always better to have the reviews written directly on the specific review sites like the ones listed above.

There is one huge rule to asking for reviews online: Never offer any incentive for a positive review. This type of influence is against the terms of use policy for quality review sites and can do more harm than good. By offering any payback for a positive review, you have opened the door to offending a customer and spreading the word that your business pays (in goods, services or money) for reviews. Doing so results in getting a reputation no honest businessperson wants.

Remember, it is absolutely critical to develop an effective process to collect positive reviews about your business, and you need to make it as easy as possible. If you just let things happen, you will either have no reviews, or worse yet the reviews written will tend to be on the negative side.

So, buying reviews is out of the question. But so is spending every waking hour working on polishing and building your online reputation. You need a workable plan. That's what's up next.

CHAPTER 7

NEXT STEPS

Overwhelmed yet? It wouldn't be modern marketing if you weren't. The days of placing an ad in the phone book were a lot simpler in some ways – but at least in the digital age, you've got more options for getting your message in front of your prospects.

It's a lot to take in. Even though this is just the tip of the iceberg for online reputation management and marketing, it's a pretty solid primer to help you get oriented.

Here are some basic, bare bones steps you can take to protect and build your online reputation:

- Set expectations on your website and social media pages. Set work hours. Post an expected response time for your site visitors. Be realistic; most people will understand you can't be available 24 hours a day. It does no good if you promise an immediate response and then don't comment for 48 hours.

- If you find you need to be available all the time, hire a customer service representative. Hiring someone to help connect with your clientele can be a positive sign of growth for your business. Analyze the situation and determine if you need to hire someone to help you manage your online reputation.

- Set some rules for the atmosphere on your page. If you want a social community that is thriving, trusting and ready to do business with you, set some ground rules around things like trust, pushy sales, name-calling and the like. Then set the example.

- If someone breaks the rules, follow through. Give a warning or remove people from your social media space. Remember, people do business with those they know, like and trust. Your social media page or group, as well as your blog, are your home on social media.

- Make it friendly, sociable and relationship-based. Showcase people helping people, whether it's through wisdom, humor or camaraderie. It's what people expect and demand online.

- Be transparent, open and honest. Showing who you are is hands-down the best business practice ever, especially online. People can't see you and shake your hand online like they can in real life.

When you are judged and examined, questioned and feared, always speak with openness, respect and kindness. Do what you say you will do. Make doing the right thing to fix a problem your only priority, not the last resort.

Can I Do This Myself or Should I Let the Pros Handle It?

Outsourcing your online reputation management can be a cost-effective move. Professional reputation management teams have developed tested systems for cranking out content, building quality links and monitoring your business. By outsourcing this task, you free up time to tend to the other aspects of your business. You have input on the content and can add posts to keep things personal and real.

Your online reputation is critical to business success. The Internet is a powerful place, and social media is an active tool to make or break a brand, especially a small business without deep pocket access to resources and tools. Hiring someone experienced in social media is a great move.

Hiring an Online Reputation Management Provider

Let's say you've made the decision to hire an Online Reputation Management (ORP) provider. How do you decide who is best for your needs? You want a company that looks into different aspects of your business.

What stage of business are you in right now? Are you a startup or an established business? ORP providers often specialize in different sizes and types of companies. Find one willing to take the time to get to know you, especially if they are in another city. If they aren't willing to come see you, or meet with you over Skype or Facetime to get to know what you're all about, they aren't the best provider for you.

What is your marketing strategy? How do your customers find you? Will the Online Reputation Management (ORM) company you are considering take you on if you are brick and mortar or solely online? In what ways will they connect with your clients and potential customers to increase your traffic?

What's their pricing strategy? It is not unusual to invest $400 a week if you are a small business or up to $3200 per week for a large business. Some companies will offer an a la carte menu of services along with a full package of reputation building and protection. Maybe all you need is market research or an email newsletter. You can find a company that will provide these services independent of a full-scale contract.

Don't be afraid to take a little time to find the right ORM provider for your business. You need a good fit when you choose to trust this company with your reputation. Investing the time and money into proper online reputation management will more than pay for itself by drawing in new and repeat customers for years.

Online Reputation Management Is Never Done

Being 'finished' with online reputation management isn't possible. The Internet is a wide-open world and things are always changing. The only way to maintain your good name online is to put in the maintenance time.

Investigating, monitoring and enhancing your online reputation needs to be part of your daily routine and a priority for your marketing budget. Get started today and see how online reputation management can change the course of your business. Your bottom line will be coming up, up, up sooner than you hoped possible.

ABOUT THE AUTHORS

Ken Tucker
Founder, Changescape Web
www.ChangescapeWeb.com
Ken@ChangescapeWeb.com

Ken Tucker is the founder of Changescape Web (www.changescapeweb.com), a Small Business Marketing and Website Design Agency. Changescape Web specializes in developing comprehensive integrated marketing strategy and campaigns for small and mid-sized businesses across the Midwest.

Ken is a Master Duct Tape Consultant (since 2015) and an Inbound Marketing Certified Professional (since 2010). He serves as the chief marketing strategist for Changescape Web, which he founded in 2005.

He also provides training in the Duct Tape Marketing System and Social Media as well as offering a complete range of marketing, advertising and strategy services.

He taught Social Media Marketing and Content Management Systems at the St. Charles Community College for 5 years (from 2011 – 2016).

Ken currently serves as Co-Chair of the St. Charles County Chambers of Commerce Technology Committee and is on the Board of Directors for the Greater St. Charles County Chamber. He speaks to chambers and business organizations on topics such as marketing strategy, online marketing, social media marketing, and local search engine optimization.

Follow Ken Tucker:
www.twitter.com/changescape
www.linkedin.com/in/kentuckerweb
www.plus.google.com/+Changescapeweb

Special Offers from Ken:
Changescape Web Can Help Your Business Improve Its SEO
Do you wonder how your website is doing against competitors? We offer a complimentary Competitive Search Rank Report – for 20 keyword phrases against 3 competitors. And we'll run a reputation report for you.

Visit http://changescapeweb.com/competitive-search-rank-report/ and complete the information in the form. We will create the report and scheduled a time with you to review your results.

Changescape Web is available to your organization to speak on a variety of topics related to Marketing Systems, Social Media, Inbound Marketing and Online Marketing. Visit our website to learn more and to book Ken as a speaker. http://changescapeweb.com/professional-speakers/

 **Ray L. Perry** is a marketing consultant, business advisor and author of *"Guide to Marketing your Business Online"* (2011), and co-author of *"Renewable Referrals"* (2014), *"The Small Business Owners Guide to Local Lead Generation"* (2015), *"Do Leadership: A step-by-step Guide to Doing Thought Leadership"* (2016) and the soon to be released *"Avid Strategy: How Focus, Culture and Commitment can grow your Small Business"* (2017).

Ray is also the co-author of the *"Marketing Guides for Small Business"* eBook series, which includes topics on Website Design, Local SEO, Google AdWords, Social Media, Content Marketing, and Reputation Management. Ray is also a featured author on Duct Tape Publishing. To learn more about Ray's books visit **www.amazon.com/author/rayperry**.

Ray is the Founder and Chief Marketing Officer of MarketBlazer, Inc., a technology based marketing agency specializing in small business lead generation, lead conversion, and customer engagement. Ray brings to the MarketBlazer team nearly three decades of leadership expertise in operations, sales, and marketing of technology products and services within start-up and high-growth entrepreneurial environments. With over 25 years of senior sales and marketing experience coupled with C level management experience, Ray understands the marketing process and its role in supporting the growth of small businesses. MarketBlazer combines a proven 7 step marketing framework and strong technology background with the latest marketing tactics, including online marketing, content marketing and social media marketing to develop solid long-term inbound marketing strategies for clients. The

MarketBlazer goal with marketing is simple and straight forward; **To help our clients' business thrive.** To learn more about improving your small business marketing and working with MarketBlazer visit **www.MarketBlazer.com.**

Ray is a Master Marketing Consultant certified by Duct Tape Marketing. Visit **www.NeedMarketing.com** to learn more about the benefits of hiring a Master Marketing Consultant certified by Duct Tape Marketing. Ray is also a StoryBrand Certified Copywriter, specializing in developing engaging content marketing strategies and a Digital Marketer Certified Customer Value Optimization Specialist, specializing in developing optimized sales funnels for generating higher quality leads at a lower acquisition cost.

Follow Ray L. Perry:

www.twitter.com/raylperry
www.linkedin.com/in/raylperry
www.plus.google.com/+rayperry

Learn more about Ray's Books:

www.amazon.com/author/rayperry
www.raylperry.com

Special Offers from Ray:

Free SEO Analysis:

Now more than ever, having an effective online presence for your business is a necessity. Setting your business up to be found in the search engines is a great way to expose your brand or business to new potential customers.

Our free SEO analysis tool can help you identify key issues on your website that may be preventing you from achieving high rankings in organic search. Our SEO analysis provides information on the most important aspects of your website.

Enter your website details for a free, no obligation SEO analysis of your website today!

www.marketblazer.com/resources/seo-analysis

Small Business Marketing Audit:

The MarketBlazer Business Marketing Audit is a valuable tool that measures the effectiveness of your existing Marketing Strategy guided by the proven methods of the Duct Tape Marketing System and the *"7 Steps to Small Business Marketing Success"*. As a Master Marketing Consultant certified by Duct Tape Marketing, MarketBlazer believes firmly in Strategy before Tactics.

After completing the Business Marketing Audit and review session meeting with Ray, you will leave the meeting with at least 3 to 5 actionable marketing tactics to improve your marketing effectiveness.

www.marketblazer.com/resources/business-marketing-audit

Phil Singleton

Kansas City Web Design®
www.KCWebDesigner.com
Kansas City SEO®
www.KCSEOPro.com

Phil Singleton is a self-described 'SEO grunt' obsessed with tweaking websites for search engine optimization and functional performance. Phil is a Duct Tape Marketing Certified Consultant and has a B.S. In Finance from Fairfield University and an MBA from Thunderbird, The Graduate School of International Management in Phoenix, Arizona.

Phil is co-author author of the Amazon best-seller *The Small Business Owner's Guide To Local Lead Generation* **(2015), and author of the Amazon best-selling Kindle eBook** *How To Hire A Web Designer: And Not Get Burned By Another Agency* **(2015). Phil is also co-author of the upcoming book** *"Top Ten Marketing Tactics"* **(2016).**

A finance guy by training, Phil is laser-focused on ROI and passionate about helping companies generate more phone call leads, email inquiries and referral business. Small business marketing consulting, with a focus on web design and SEO, is just a means to this end. Phil believes that the Internet drives more purchase decisions than any other medium in history of capitalism, and as such has devoted the last fifteen years to working with companies of all sizes to significantly improve their search engine visibility. In addition to providing inbound marketing consulting services to companies in the Midwest and nationally, Phil provides SEO-friendly custom WordPress & Magento websites under the brand Kansas City Web Design® (www.kcwebdesigner.com) and online marketing and search engine optimization services under the brand Kansas City SEO® (**www.kcseopro.com**).

Phil is an active blogger and his content and blog posts have been featured on Duct Tape Marketing, Freshbooks.com, SEMRush.com, Ahrefs.com, AdvancedWebRanking.com & WebDesignerDepot.com and many local Kansas City and Midwest regional print publications and websites. Some highlights of Phil's unique career:

- Helped dozens of US startups and tech companies raise millions of dollars in strategic venture capital investment and cross-border licensing agreements in the Asia Pacific region.

- Ran the global retail and online sales divisions for a best-selling line of consumer software products.

- Started a software company in Asia, raising over $1M in venture capital funding, grew to profitability with 25 employees, then sold three years later. This experience in what got him into SEO and Internet marketing…in short by following the ROI trail to SEO.

- Is fluent in Mandarin Chinese

- Lived in Asia for over 10 years, primarily in Taipei, Taiwan, and briefly in Beijing, Shanghai & Hong Kong. Traveled extensively throughout the Asia-Pacific region on business.

- Lives in Overland Park, KS with wife Vivian and twin sons Ely & Ostyn.

Follow Phil Singleton:

https://twitter.com/kcwebsites
https://plus.google.com/+PhilSingleton

https://www.linkedin.com/in/seokansascity
Learn More About Phil's Books
http://www.amazon.com/author/philsingleton

Special Offers from Phil:

Free SEO Website Audit

Get a detailed SEO website on your website today. You will not only receive a detailed report on your website, but an electronic copy of the Amazon best-seller: *"How To Hire A Web Designer: And Not Get Burned By Another Agency."*

Get your free one-click SEO report here:

http://websitereview.kcseopro.com